Also by Robb Pearlman

Spoiler Alert: Bruce Willis Is Dead and 399 More Endings from Movies, TV, Books, and Life

NERD HAIKU

Robb Pearlman

LYONS PRESS
Guilford, Connecticut

An imprint of Globe Pequot Press

To buy books in quantity for corporate use
or incentives, call **(800) 962-0973**
or e-mail **premiums@GlobePequot.com.**

Lyons Press is an imprint of Globe Pequot Press.

Layout: Joanna Beyer
Project editor: Kristen Mellitt

Library of Congress Cataloging-in-Publication Data is available on file.

ISBN 978-0-7627-8043-3

Printed in the United States of America

10 9 8 7 6 5 4 3 2 1

Just referencing the
Comic Book Guy makes this the
Best. Haiku. Ever.

Anticipation.
Heady thrill of not knowing.
Mmm, blind packaging.

Wednesday's too far in
the space-time continuum.
New comic book day.

**There's nothing quite like
Shakespeare in original
Klingon. Classic lit.**

I support local
independent booksellers.
"Large skim latte, please."

Kane, Schuster, Siegel, Lee, Kirby, Fox, and Finger, these are names to know.

Gelflings and Hobbits
should, in theory, be besties,
but I could be wrong.

Vampires/Buffy,
The Walking Dead/well-placed ax.
It's a yin-yang thing.

X-Men/Magneto,
JLA/Darkseid. Can't we
all just get along?

Who's faster, the Flash
or Superman? This is a
debate without end.

Eight Words: Doomed planet. Desperate Scientists. Last Hope. Kindly Couple.

Jason, Damian,
and Stephanie can all just
kiss Dick Grayson's ass.

Batwoman won't work
Fridays after sundown or
on Rosh Hashanah.

He's responsible
for more square miles than them all.
Don't dis Aquaman.

The Royal Flush Gang
doesn't know what happens there's
supposed to stay there.

**Widow, Cat, Panther
Bolt, Lightning, or Canary,
Black is beautiful.**

**It's a well-known fact:
Cyclops is kind of a douche.
Jean Grey has bad taste.**

Red Skull is Elrond
is Mr. Smith. What thread is
this Hugo Weaving?

Does *everything* stretch?
    'Cause you could make mad money,
              Mr. Fantastic.

Reed Richards, meet Eel

O'Brian   and   Ralph   Dibny.

Oh,   it's   on,   bitches.

Robb Pearlman

If I had a type,
I'd say simple and carefree:
Comic Sans Serif.

**Nobody believes
me. That's what happens when you
date Sue Storm Richards.**

Saved the universe,
but I'm totally bummed out.
Girlfriend's in the fridge.

 13

My asthma kicks in
and I throw up in my mouth.
Girl in comic store.

**Wish I lived before
Comics Code Authority
made skirts much longer.**

Ororo Munroe
and Mari Jiwe McCabe,
my African queens.

**Every day it goes
where no man has gone before,
Uhura's earpiece.**

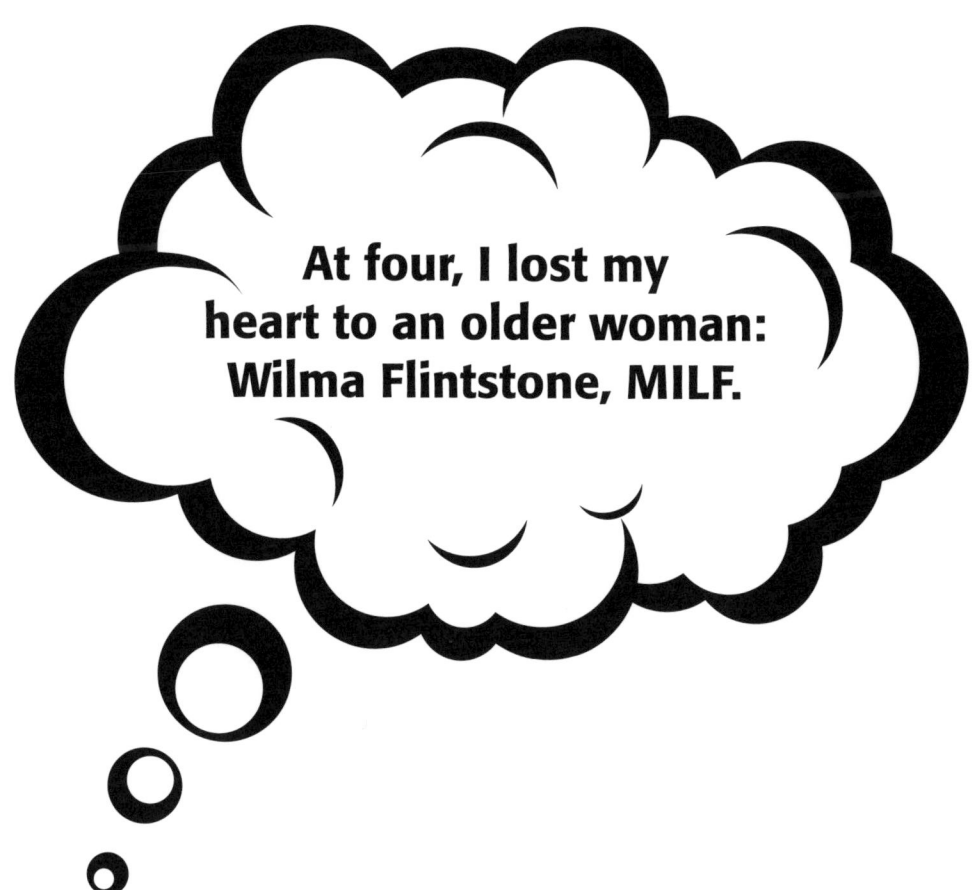

At four, I lost my
heart to an older woman:
Wilma Flintstone, MILF.

Someday we will find
the right vehicle for you,
Eliza Dushku.

**From my perspective,
panties have firewalls that are
password protected.**

**She stopped before she
touched me down there. Again, life
has blocked my pop-up.**

When we get girlfriends,
many things will change for us.
Yeah, wishful thinking.

**Virgin. Gamer. I
try to vary things, but still
my right arm's bigger.**

So much changed after
you got laid, but I'm the same.
Crisis on my Earth.

Eartha, Halle, Anne,

Lee, Julie, Michelle—I get

a lot of pussy.

7 of 9 +
BSG's 6 = fun.
(I majored in math.)

From Ms. Pac Man to
Ms. Lara Croft, Title IX
funding FTW!

**You're such a nice girl.
Please don't disappear** on me
like Kitty **Pryde did.**

A pat excuse not
to date me, but guess what: I
am Y, the Last Man!

Took thirty years, but
I have a new girlfriend. Thanks,
MMRPG!

I like pillow talk,
like "Glasses are sexy," and
"Go get 'em, Tiger."

I see Valeris.
Girlfriend sees Samantha Jones.
Sex and the City.

The buns are OK, but I really want you to dress like Slave Leia.

I love you so much
that your engagement ring will
be *The Dark Crystal.*

You made me a man,
then mixed up *Wars* and *Trek.* I'm
breaking up with you.

**Like Lana and Gwen,
you were ahead of the curve.
First girlfriend syndrome.**

I will wear a tux
and a custom fez when I
marry Amy Pond.

Regenerated
Abbot and Costello are
Doctor Who's on first.

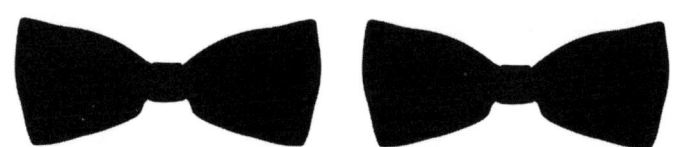

Lightsaber chopsticks turn ordinary pad thai into Padmé Thai.

**I'd go back in time
to be surprised again. "No,
I am your father."**

I'm such a badass:
Bantha skull shoulder tattoo.
Please don't tell my dad!

**Dad won't admit it,
but let's face it, my brother:
I'm Thor; you're Loki.**

Dad didn't get it.
He wanted me to play ball.
Now I own the team!

Computers are good
for more than just watching porn.
Do you hear me, Dad?

Eyes squint in daylight.
Mom still does my laundry. I
live in her basement.

**Mom wants me outside,
but then how will I know when
people read my blog?**

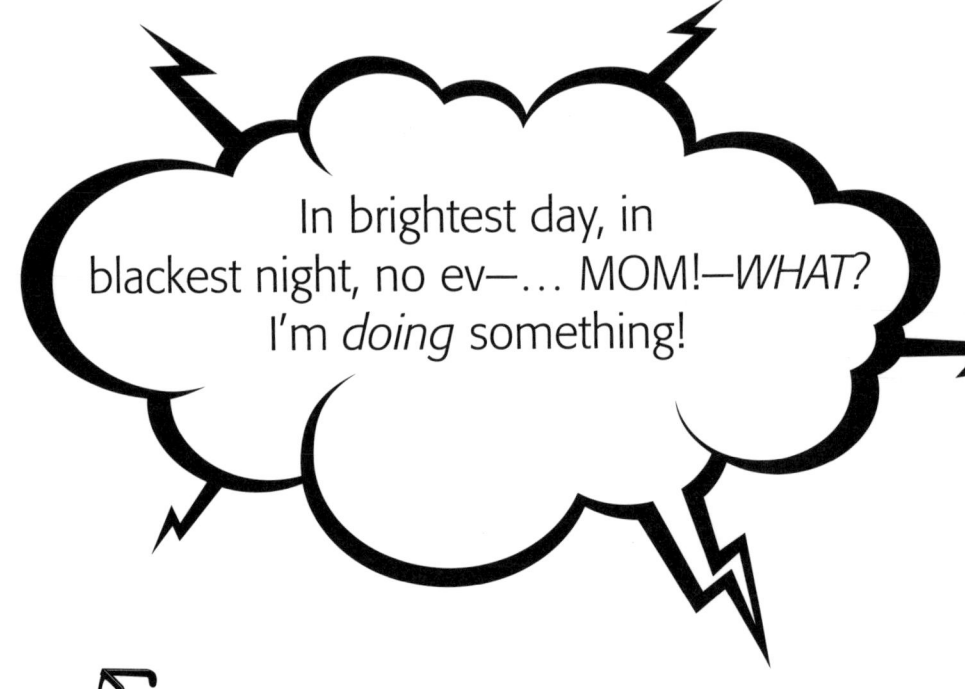

In brightest day, in
blackest night, no ev—… MOM!—*WHAT?*
I'm *doing* something!

Thought I'd be rich now,
but my plan was thwarted when
Mom sold my comics.

Sad when Granny passed,
but was beside myself when
Mrs. Summers died.

**Asgard, Gotham, Hoth,
Middle Earth, Winterfell, Oz,
there's no place like home.**

My summer job sucks.
Days spent skimming hair away.
Pool boy on Kashyyyk.

Nothing you can say
will stop me from wearing a
T-shirt on the beach.

I can't help you move.
No, my car's totally fine.
***Star Trek* marathon.**

I never knew the
joy of musicals before
Dr. Horrible.

**I was all alone,
then your music spoke to me,
"Weird" Al Yankovic.**

Spidey on Broadway?
Suspension of disbelief
has its limits, dude.

Robb Pearlman

The birdhouse in my
soul is filled up with tweets from
They Might Be Giants.

Small apartment, but
I can really spread out here
on the holodeck.

**The Baxter Building
allows flames but not smoking.
Co-op boards are weird.**

Special packaging
on this Blu-ray set's cool but
won't fit on my shelf.

**Ikea shelves are
hard to assemble with a
sonic screwdriver.**

I yell in my sleep,
"Thunder-Thunder-Thundercats!"
My roommate hates me.

**Don't blame me for not
knowing what you mean. You do
not have thought bubbles.**

You misread the die.
He clearly rolled a twenty.
Bad Dungeon Master!

I think it's funny,
you laugh for the wrong reason.
Ironic T-shirt.

You still use Hotmail,
and you ate my Hot Pocket.
You're a bad roommate.

Yeah? Well, you know what?
I'd still hate your stupid face
over on Earth-2.

Romulans? Um, no.
Ever hear of the Borg, jerk?
Why do we hang out?

You misspoke when you
said Iron Man was a droid.
Effing idiot.

Your words can't hurt me.

Neither can your sticks and stones.
Adamantium.

Hanging with my friends,
but thanks to the Internet
I'm still all alone!

**There is nothing like
watching movies with friends on
MST3K.**

Superman made me
believe a man can fly and
dams can fall apart.

Will give it a shot,
but if the film sucks I will
so blog about it.

Camped out at theater
overnight. Twenty bucks for
IMAX. Please don't suck.

Waited in line for
two days for these seats, lady.
Shut that baby up!

RealD glasses don't
fit over my prescription.
I'm stuck with 2D.

**Not how it happened,
origin story altered.
Adaptations. Ugh.**

The trilogy just
ended. Now there's a new one?
Reboot *this,* asshole.

Chronologically
X-Men: First Class doesn't work
as a true prequel.

**Though kind of clunky,
mechanical web shooters
really do make sense.**

The blond or redhead?
For a nerd, Peter Parker
has some tough choices.

The red pill or blue?
The real choice should have been to
stop after one film.

Not stalking you, but
the sequels were really bad,
and you should know it.

Milla Jovovich
makes anything watchable.
Resident Evil.

**No cash to spare, but
I'll buy whatever is up
for Kate Beckinsale.**

There's something so right
about a movie as wrong
as *Starship Troopers.*

The day after a
Chris Nolan premiere should be
a nerd holiday.

Dead before its time.
Oh, Paramount, why did you
***Deep Space Nine* my heart?**

Basic cable's fine.
All I need are G4 and
The Big Bang Theory.

BBCA is
to Syfy as chips are to
fries. Hail, Britannia!

Thought I'd seen it all,
but Blu-ray proved me wrong. The
saga is complete.

Wrote a brilliant book.
No one sees the subtlety.
Klingon's hard to get.

**Rage and confusion.
The world is turned upside down.
Hugo Award snub.**

**The birds are singing
on this great Alderaan day!
Hey, what's that in the—**

Only member of
the Alderaan Optimists
Society. *Sigh.*

Like a Romulan
cloaking device covering
my soul, I am shy.

**Pocket protector,
you keep my chest safe and warm,
yet my heart grows cold.**

I sit on sidelines,
but unlike the quarterback
I rock at *Madden.*

**I'm not myopic,
and I play football . . . somewhere
in the Multiverse.**

You prefer games of
strength and agility. I
prefer *Game of Thrones.*

I'm well prepared for
a zombie apocalypse.
Are you, pretty boy?

Tell Ryan Seacrest
January 1st now starts
The New 52.

1, 2, tap-tap-tap.
I'm obsessive compulsive.
1, 2, tap-tap-tap.

**5 7 5 hard.
Structure too strict for art form.
Hulk no like haiku.**

Teach the children well:
4, 5, 6, 1, 2, 3 is
the way to watch them.

Star Trek movie rule:
The reboot notwithstanding,
evens are better.

Your fingers are too
fat for small touch screens. Meek shall
inherit the earth.

Feel bad for Pluto.
His master's a mouse, and now
he's not a planet.

2001 was
more Kubrick's *The Shining* than
a space odyssey.

Speech Therapist! To Dagobah must you come. Bad syntax do I have.

Robb Pearlman

Red Dead Redemption
and two piece and a biscuit.
Big Saturday night.

70

Must keep my nerd cred.
I've never played D&D.
Don't say *anything.*

Blue, round, and fast, you're
a credit to your species,
Sonic the Hedgehog.

**Allergic to hay,
but Farmville lets me claim that
I am outdoorsy.**

My fear of Mott's stems,
over the rainbow, from those
apple trees in Oz.

It's lonely, but it's
better to be feared than loved.
My *World of Warcraft.*

Game Stop offered me
a job because I know more
than the current staff.

Desktop ruled by a
fully articulated
Cobra Commander.

Professional with
an obscure quote at the end.
My email footer.

Matthew Broderick,
global thermonuclear
war. Career path set.

00110101
00110111
(Binary Haiku)

⏻

You need IT help?
OK, one question for you:
Did you turn it on?

No login needed,
so what I really mean is
You. Shall. Not. Password!

Skynet stock will climb
before plummeting along
with humanity.

Toasters were harmless.
Battlestar Galactica
changed all that for me.

It's the new iPhone,
not the Droid, I'm looking for
in this year's stocking.

Learned how to drive a
stick and customize just to
steer Optimus Prime.

**Starship *Enterprise,*
the *Millennium Falcon.*
I have . . . a Honda.**

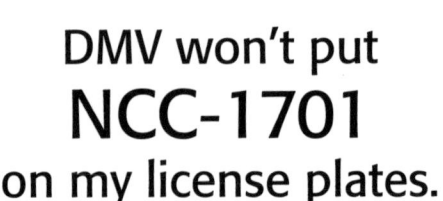

DMV won't put
NCC-1701
on my license plates.

A hybrid car, hmm?
Does it come loaded with a
flux capacitor?

**The Go-Bots are the
Hydrox to the Transformers'
Oreo cookies.**

Robb Pearlman

Harley Davidson
could get nerds on a hog with
a Tron Light Cycle.

86

Barbara Gordon and
Professor Xavier
get great parking spots.

Sure, he can fix a
flat, but can he speak Elvish?
I didn't think so.

Hippocratic Oath,
yet Kaylee's feelings were hurt.
Doctor Simon Tam.

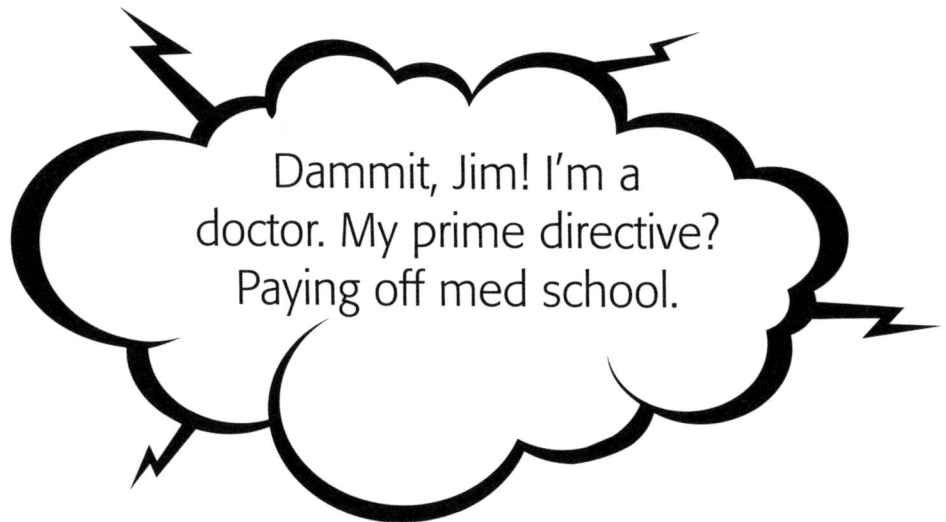

Dammit, Jim! I'm a
doctor. My prime directive?
Paying off med school.

Who needs a degree?
All you need are snacks and a
Mystery Machine.

**Your plan went awry.
You forgot to account for
us meddling kids. Zoinks!**

Saturday mornings
I wake up early to play
with my Super Friends.

I can watch Tweety
again and again. But the
Raven? Nevermore.

Robb Pearlman

Spidey, Lucius, and *The Electric Company* taught me how to spell.

Searching for a word
that will bring you to your knees.
Scrabble tournament.

Forgot *vacuum* has
two *us*. Space and spelling bee
judges abhor me.

Robb Pearlman

In retrospect, six
was just a little young to
see *The Exorcist.*

The kids may not care,
but you and I both know that
Han shot Greedo first.

Hours in line, but
heatstroke will not keep me from
Star Tours at Disney.

**You want to sound like
a droid or alien? Use
a British accent.**

Taking the Great Dane
to the Ren Fair. It's OK,
the saddle fits him.

Maybe my cat's name
is Schrödinger. Or is it?
We will never know.

Highly allergic,
I named my pet fish Krypto.
It's just not the same.

**I am the only
one here wearing a red shirt.
This will not end well.**

That didn't work out.
Things got really out of hand.
I need a Time Lord.

I wear a bow tie
because you think it is cool,
Eleventh Doctor.

Tuxedo T-shirt
and new Chuck Taylors for the
black-tie reception.

Holds my iPhone *and*
Blackberry. Real leather, too.
Utility belt.

Question: Why do I knit Cthulhu hats? Answer: Because I Lovecrafts.

Blue blazer over
Super Grover T-shirt is
business casual.

Juicy Juice and some
Smurfberry Crunch are just part
of a good breakfast.

Better than coffee,
bigger jolt than Red Bull: the
power of Grayskull!

Spilled soup all over,
but this fur is forgiving.
Dressed like a Wookie.

**I spent every dime
for this Cosplay masquerade.
Put on the damn cape.**

My costume cost more
than I spent on food last year.
Take my picture. Please.

I feel tall and thin
and socially adjusted.
I like ComicCon.

ComicCon's the place
where I can achieve my dream:
Do Wonder Woman.

I'm bald, so costume
choices are limited to
Picard or Luthor.

**Uploads take too long,
and there's a line for nachos.
Too many nerds here.**

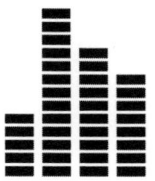

Thank you, E.T., but
no Reese's Pieces for me.
Peanut allergy.

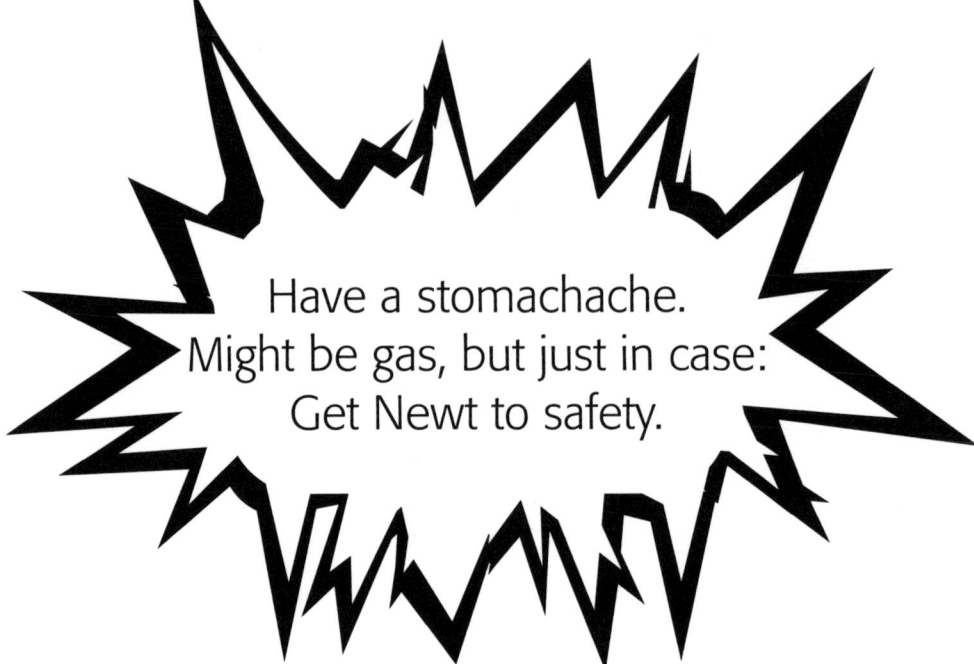

Have a stomachache.
Might be gas, but just in case:
Get Newt to safety.

Telemarketers?
I would much rather get the
Call of Cthulhu.

Hey, Rupe? Perry White
and J. Jonah Jameson
would never hack phones.

Maester, not *master.*
Lannister, not *banister.*
Damn autocorrect.

**Can't sleep, wondering:
Will werewolves or mermaids be
the next vampires?**

The only teams I
wasn't picked last for were Teams
Edward and Jacob.

Wolverine kicks ass.
Adamantium *and* 'tude?
I'd go gay for him.

The hottest part of
Scott Pilgrim vs. the World?
Not all boy exes.

Frodo and Samwise,
Archie and Jughead, too. Guys,
it's time to come out.

**Keep your Robin Hood.
I can do you one better:
the man they call Jayne.**

**With great power comes
great responsibility?
Way too much pressure.**

**Dear Housekeeping: Please
vacuum under the bed, too.
I may have Tribbles.**

I never go down
to the basement for laundry.
The C.H.U.Ds will get me.

OK, I get that
"Knowing is half the battle."
What's the other half?

I refuse to eat
50-year-old Soylent Green.
Too many hormones.

LARPing sounds stranger
than live-action role-playing,
but it saves me time.

Martin needs more time?
He had better hurry up.
Winter is coming.

**Early adopter,
I'm now suffering from bad
newer gen envy.**

When I go shopping,
I wait for back-to-school sales
on Diagon Alley.

Out of the way, kid.
This toy's marketed to the
adult collector.

The cutest little
Sith Lord from here to Nabu.
Lego Darth Vader.

Santa, take me to
the Island of Misfit Toys.
It's where I belong.

So we're just supposed
to forget the Smoke Monster?
I still don't get it.

Too long to explain.
Netflix all of the seasons,
and then we can talk.

Things don't always make
sense, like poverty, crime, or
invisible jets.

Done writing this book.

Won't go back to make changes.

Lucas reference!

I'd like to thank the
below, but not in haiku.
This nerd's exhausted.

Ethan Collings, Jessica Fuller, David Harmon, Gene Hult, Jono Jarrett, James Jayo, Linda Kaplan, Nellie Kurtzman, Linda Pricci, Mary Robinson, David Rosen, Mitchell Waters, Leah Whisler, and all of the writers, artists, creators, Jedi, Federation Officers, Time Lords, Hobbits, Kryptonians, and Asgardians who give us something to live for.